PIANO / VOCAL / GUITAR

LADIES OF SONG

INSPIRING BALLADS & ROMANTIC STANDARDS SUNG BY GREAT FEMALE VOCALISTS

T0066621

On the cover:
Sarah Vaughan, Judy Garland, Julie London,
Ella Fitzgerald, Kay Starr, Rosemary Clooney

Photos of Rosemary Clooney
courtesy of Michael Ochs Archives/Getty.

Photos of Shirley Horn
courtesy of Larry Busacca.

Photos of Betty Carter, June Christy, Petula Clark, Natalie Cole,
Chris Conner, Doris Day, Blossom Dearie, Ruth Etting, Judy Garland, Etta James, Joni James, Peggy Lee,
Susannah McCorkle, Carmen McRae, Ethel Merman, Bette Midler, Liza Minnelli, Dianne Reeves, Linda Ronstadt,
Dinah Shore, Nina Simone, Keely Smith, Kay Starr, Sarah Vaughan, Margaret Whiting
courtesy of Photofest.

Photos of Ella Fitzgerald, Roberta Flack, Astrud Gilberto, Eydie Gormé, Billie Holiday,
Lena Horne, Julie London, Helen O'Connell, Anita O'Day, Patti Page, Jo Stafford, Barbra Streisand,
Dionne Warwick, Dinah Washington, Nancy Wilson
courtesy of William "PoPsie" Randolph.
www.PoPsiePhotos.com

ISBN 978-1-4234-8898-9

HAL•LEONARD®
CORPORATION
7777 W. BLUEMOUND RD. P.O. BOX 13819 MILWAUKEE, WI 53213

Visit Hal Leonard Online at
www.halleonard.com

CONTENTS

SINGER INDEX

LADIES OF SONG
THE BIOGRAPHIES

BETTY CARTER (1929-1998)

Born in Flint, Michigan, Lillie Mae Jones began studying piano in Detroit as a young girl. By the time she was in her teens, she was sitting in with the likes of Charlie Parker and Miles Davis when they were in town. She turned pro at sixteen and by eighteen was working with Lionel Hampton's band as Lorraine Carter. Hampton dubbed her "Betty Be-Bop," in a reference to her free-spirited, acrobatic scat singing. Despite a strong start, and her abilities as a pianist and arranger, Carter's career suffered the same slump most jazz singers experienced in the '60s and '70s. She established her own recording company, Bet-Car Productions in 1970, and produced some of her best recordings there. She signed with Verve in 1987 and saw an enormous resurgence of her popularity in the last decade of her life. She won a GRAMMY® in 1980 and a National Medal of Arts in 1994.

JUNE CHRISTY (1925-1990)

Born Shirley Luster, in Springfield, Illinois, June Christy spent most of her childhood in Iowa. She began singing in her early teens, working with a Decatur "society band," playing weddings, parties and the like. She left home after high school and moved to Chicago, taking the name Sharon Leslie. In 1945 she won an audition for a spot with the Stan Kenton band, scoring numerous hits with the band. She began recording on her own in 1947, eventually turning out recordings that had an enormous impact on the cool jazz scene of the 1950s. Yet critics, fans and the singer herself debated whether she was a jazz or pop singer. Christy largely retired from performing in 1965, making one final recording in the late 1970s.

PETULA CLARK
(B. 1932)

Born in Surrey, England, Petula Sally Olwen Clark began her career as a radio entertainer in Britain during World War II. Still active into the new millennium, Clark has maintained a career that spans more than seventy years. She scored hits on both sides of the Atlantic, including "Downtown," which was released in four languages in 1964 and went straight to the top of the U.S. charts, reviving her then slumping career. Clark put forty consecutive songs on the U.S. Top 40 chart and won two GRAMMY awards. She made thirty films, and won accolades for her theater work both in London's West End and on Broadway. She wrote the score for the West End show *Someone Like You* in the late 1980s and made her Broadway debut in 1993 in *Blood Brothers*. Her recording of "Downtown" was inducted into the Grammy Hall of Fame in 2003.

ROSEMARY CLOONEY
(1928-2002)

Raised in poverty in Kentucky, Rosemary and her sister Betty were left to fend for themselves as teenagers. The girls won a singing contest, which led to a regular gig in Cincinnati. The sisters worked with Tony Pastor's band for several years, until Betty returned to Cincinnati and Rosemary headed for New York. Rosemary hit the national scene just as the American public developed a taste for the sound of "girl singers." Her dark, warm voice and thoughtful song interpretations made her an instant hit. She built a career that included films now deemed classics, including *White Christmas*, and unforgettable recordings. There were tragedies too, including the day in 1968 when she was standing just yards from presidential candidate Bobby Kennedy when he was assassinated. Clooney, the aunt of actor George Clooney, received a Lifetime Achievement GRAMMY in 2002.

NATALIE COLE
(B. 1950)

Natalie Marie Cole, the daughter of singer Nat "King" Cole, was born in Los Angeles. She made her first recording at age six, singing on her father's Christmas album. She began performing at age eleven. A singer and songwriter in her own right, Cole began in R&B but moved into smooth jazz. She left the spotlight for a time in the 1980s to deal with a drug problem. Her recordings, which have won nine GRAMMY awards as of 2009, include an album of her own arrangements of her father's hits and an album of covers previously recorded by such greats as Dinah Washington, Nina Simone and Sarah Vaughan. Cole has also enjoyed a career as an actress, appearing on television in such shows as *Law & Order: Special Victims Unit* and *Grey's Anatomy*.

CHRIS CONNOR
(B. 1927)

Kansas City native Chris Connor started out on the clarinet as a child, but became known for her dark, rich voice, and nuanced vocal style. In 1952 she realized her dream of singing with Stan Kenton's band, making a national name for herself in the process. She recorded with Atlantic Records until 1962. After moving to the short-lived FM Records in the 1960s, Connor began touring Japan and recording on the Japanese label Alfa. She maintained a devoted following and continued recording for various labels throughout the '70s and '80s and was still touring in the '90s. The turn of the new century found Connor recording for the New York-based High Note Records. In 2003 Connor and pianist/arranger Dave Matthews released an album named after one of her signature songs, George Shearing's "Lullaby of Birdland," on the Japanese label King Record Co.

DORIS DAY
(B. 1924)

Doris Mary Ann von Kappelhoff of Cincinnati created one of the most wholesome images the entertainment industry has ever known. She began singing at age sixteen, and was soon touring with the Les Brown Band. A last minute gig, singing at a party at the home of Jule Styne, landed her a role in the film *Romance on the High Seas*. The film introduced her to the American public, who loved her. She became a tremendously popular actress and singer, dubbed by the press, "The Tomboy with a Voice," known for her scrubbed, girl-next-door image. Between 1948 and 1958, Day put fifty-four songs into the Top 30. Her biggest hit, "Sentimental Journey," resided in the #1 spot for nine weeks. She's also known for her tireless work for animal rights.

BLOSSOM DEARIE
(1926-2009)

In a business full of clever stage names, Blossom Dearie used her unique given name to build an international career. Born of Norwegian descent in upstate New York, Dearie moved to New York City after high school and began a career as a jazz pianist. She began recording as a singer in the late 1950s. A 1962 jingle recorded for Hires Root Beer led to an album that could be mail-ordered for a dollar and a Hires bottle cap. She built a following in the U.S. and London, creating her own record label, Daffodil, in 1974. She lent her voice to the animated television series *Schoolhouse Rock!* (1973-1985). Dearie's high, facile voice and touchingly vulnerable sound have kept her in demand, at places like Danny's Skylight Room in New York, into the new millennium.

RUTH ETTING
(1897-1978)

Known as "America's Sweetheart of Song," Ruth Etting left her home in David City, Nebraska at age seventeen, and headed to art school in Chicago. She went quickly from designing costumes for nightclub chorus girls to joining the chorus line herself and was soon heard on the radio and in recordings on the Columbia label. She first appeared on Broadway in the *Ziegfeld Follies of 1927*, making several short films in the 1930s. Her career was ended in the late '30s by a famous scandal in which her mobster ex-husband, Moe "The Gimp" Snyder, shot and injured her pianist/boyfriend and was sent to jail for attempted murder. Etting, a great beauty and master of the torch song, had more than sixty hits between 1926 and 1937, several of them hitting the #1 spot. She was inducted into the GRAMMY Hall of Fame in 2005.

ELLA FITZGERALD
(1917-1996)

Young Ella Jane Fitzgerald didn't want to sing—she wanted to dance. But a bad case of stage fright at an amateur night at the New York's Apollo Theatre left her unable to dance. Instead, she grabbed a microphone, sang a song and took home the prize. America's "First Lady of Song" was born. A three-octave vocal range and an infallible musical sense gave her a six-decade career and won her thirteen GRAMMY Awards, a GRAMMY Lifetime Achievement Award and a host of other honors. She led her own orchestra and recorded at a feverish pace, on such labels as Decca, Verve, Capitol, Reprise, Atlantic and Columbia. She did a few film roles and made television appearances, the most famous of which was paid for by Memorex. "Is it live, or is it Memorex?" a voice asked as Ella's voice shattered a glass. It didn't matter—it was Ella.

ROBERTA FLACK
(B. 1937)

Born in Asheville, North Carolina and raised in Virginia, Roberta Flack graduated from Howard University at age nineteen, having received a full scholarship in classical piano. She entered graduate school in music, but left to take a teaching job after her father died. She played as a sideline, accompanying classical singers at the piano and accompanying herself while singing blues, pop and jazz. Her singing was noticed in the late 1960s, winning her a recording contract. She hit the big time when her silky rendition of "The First Time Ever I Saw Your Face" was used in Clint Eastwood's first directorial project, *Play Misty for Me*. The song hit the #1 spot in 1972 and earned her one of her four GRAMMY awards. Flack received a star on the Hollywood Walk of Fame in 1999 and was back in the recording studio in 2009.

JUDY GARLAND
(1922-1969)

Francis Ethel Gumm, dubbed "Baby" by her vaudevillian parents, made her stage debut at age two-and-a-half, singing with her sisters. Taking the name Judy from a pop song, the young performer signed a contract with MGM in 1935, landing her signature role in *The Wizard of Oz* in 1939. That performance won her a Special Achievement Academy Award®. Garland's distinctive voice won her two GRAMMY Awards and a GRAMMY Lifetime Achievement Award. When a string of issues ended her relationship with MGM, Garland began appearing in wildly successful live performances in Europe and the U.S. Garland's last years were filled with personal and health issues, ending in her death by accidental overdose in London at age forty-seven.

ASTRUD GILBERTO
(B. 1940)

Astrud Weinert was born in Brazil to German and Brazilian parents and grew up in Rio de Janeiro. She was an amateur singer when her husband, João Gilberto, suggested that she sing on a recording he was making with Stan Getz and Antonio Carlos Jobim. The bossa nova number "The Girl from Ipanema," which appeared on that album, became an international hit and reached the #5 spot in the U.S. Astrud Gilberto's professional career had begun. She was soon known as "The Girl from Ipanema" and as "The Queen of Bossa Nova." She recorded songs in several languages, including Portuguese, German and Japanese, and brought her sensual, Brazilian style of singing to all of her recordings. She was the voice of Eastern Airlines for many years and was inducted into the International Latin Music Hall of Fame in 1992.

EYDIE GORMÉ
(B. 1931)

Born Edith Gormezano in the Bronx, New York, Eydie Gormé made her radio debut at age three. She worked with husband Steve Lawrence on Steve Allen's original *Tonight Show*, performed on Broadway, headlined in major U.S. nightclubs and put pop and Latin hits on the charts. The 1964 British Invasion of the American music scene marked the last time Gormé or her husband would appear on the Billboard Top 40 chart. Fluent in Spanish, Gormé made her way into the Latin music scene, working with Trio Los Panchos. She won two GRAMMY awards during the 1960s, and received two GRAMMY nominations in the 1970s, both for Latin recordings. She won an Emmy® and, with Lawrence, was honored by the Songwriters Hall of Fame for lifetime contribution, as well as by the Film Advisory Board for their salute to Cole Porter.

BILLIE HOLIDAY
(1915-1959)

Billie Holiday, also known as "Lady Day" or the "Queen of Song," was born Eleanora Fagan in Philadelphia. Her pioneering vocal style, which drew heavily from the work of jazz instrumentalists, still influences American jazz and pop singing today. Her life was hard. She worked in a brothel, spent some time in jail and was impoverished when she began singing for tips. Her life was a mix of critical acclaim, personal problems, substance abuse and arrests. Cheated out of the profits of her recordings, she died nearly penniless, still in trouble with the law. Holiday was inducted posthumously into the Grammy Hall of Fame, established to honor a recording of "qualitative or historical significance" at least twenty-five years old. She received the award five times and received four posthumous GRAMMY awards for Best Historical Album.

SHIRLEY HORN
(1934-2005)

Washington, D.C. native Shirley Horn began playing the piano at age four and started formal lessons a year later. Her mother often had to work hard to get her daughter away from the piano to play with other children. At age twelve Horn began studying composition at Howard University. When she was eighteen she won a scholarship to Juilliard, but couldn't afford to live in New York City and had to decline. She began her singing career in Washington, D.C., going to New York for a time in 1960. When jazz musician Miles Davis heard Horn's contralto voice and intimate style of singing, he brought her to the Village Vanguard in New York, which proved to be her big break. She went back to Washington, D.C. for a time to raise her daughter, but returned to the national scene in 1978, receiving a GRAMMY in 1999.

LENA HORNE
(B. 1917)

Born in the Bedford-Stuyvesant section of Brooklyn, singer/actress Lena Horne left high school before earning her diploma. She tried her hand at films in the 1950s. Finding herself blacklisted for her political opinions, she left Hollywood and began performing in nightclubs, eventually becoming one of the top performers on the nightclub circuits of North America and Europe and garnering a Tony® nomination for her work in *Calypso*. A tireless fighter for civil rights, Horne retired from performing in 1980, but she was back in less than a year's time, winning a special Tony® and two GRAMMY awards. In the 1990s Horne made several recordings, stepping into the studio one last time in 2000 before retiring from public life.

ETTA JAMES
(B. 1938)

Los Angeles native Jamesetta Hawkins was just fourteen when she was discovered by bandleader Johnny Otis. In 1954 he arranged for James' first recording, as part of the group The Peaches. That recording of "The Wallflower (Dance with Me, Henry)" went to the top of the R&B charts in 1955. James has been successful with an enormous range of material, including rock, blues, jazz, soul, rockabilly and pop, scoring hits on the various charts over the years. She won three GRAMMY Awards, two for blues recordings and one for jazz, and received a Lifetime Achievement GRAMMY in 2003. She was inducted into the Rock and Roll Hall of Fame in 1993. James has continued working and recording, releasing an album entitled *All the Way* in 2006, which included such diverse tunes as Prince's "Purple Rain," John Lennon's "Imagine," and "Somewhere" from *West Side Story*.

JONI JAMES
(B. 1930)

Born in Chicago, Giovanna Carmella Babbo grew up in poverty after losing her father at age five. She attended Catholic schools and sang in choirs. James had a dream of becoming a ballet dancer, which she followed until an appendectomy in college slowed her down. Her life changed course when she filled in for a singer friend going on her honeymoon, and after that began to work steadily as a singer. Her break came when an MGM executive heard her singing a commercial on Chicago radio. She became one of the first artists to record country songs in a pop vein. She retired in the mid '60s to care for her ailing husband. More than a decade after his death, she remarried. Her new husband encouraged her to sing again, which led to singing for sold-out houses at venues such as Lincoln Center and Carnegie Hall.

PEGGY LEE
(1920-2002)

Born Norma Deloris Egstrom in North Dakota, Peggy Lee began her singing career on local radio before striking out for Los Angeles at age seventeen. A North Dakota program director gave her the stage name by which she would become famous as a singer/actress. She was also a songwriter, writing some of her own material and co-writing the songs to the Disney film *Lady and the Tramp* with Francis "Sonny" Burke. She brought her cool style and breezy sound to several of the film's animated characters. Lee was nominated for twelve GRAMMY Awards, winning one in 1969 and receiving a Lifetime Achievement GRAMMY in 1995. She appeared in several Hollywood films, including the 1952 remake of *The Jazz Singer* and the 1955 film *Pete Kelly's Blues*.

JULIE LONDON
(1926-2000)

Gayle Peck was "born in a trunk," to vaudeville singer/hoofers Jack and Josephine Peck. The Pecks landed in Los Angeles when Gayle was in her teens. She was "discovered" by a talent agent while working as an elevator operator. Popular as a World War II pin-up girl, London was married for a time to *Dragnet* star Jack Webb. She found her niche on the nightclub circuit, where her husky voice and intimate deliveries earned her the description "the consummate cocktail siren" by author Joseph Lanza. She recorded more than thirty albums during her career, appeared on popular variety shows of the 1950s and '60s, and was seen in numerous films. She also appeared in several television series, most memorably as the head nurse on the 1970s series *Emergency*.

SUSANNAH McCORKLE
(1946-2001)

Born in Berkeley, California, jazz/pop singer Susannah Mc-Corkle was a woman of many talents. She traveled to Mexico and Europe studying languages, eventually earning a degree in Italian literature. Her fiction and non-fiction writings were published in national publications and she was known for writing her own history-packed shows, for English lyrics for Brazilian, French and Italian songs and for her repertoire of more than three thousand songs. She gave concert lectures at colleges, put together interactive workshops in music for children and won the *Stereo Review* Album of the Year award three times. Shortly before her death, she completed a CD entitled *Most Requested Songs*. McCorkle survived cancer, but battled depression for much of her life.

CARMEN McRAE
(1920-1994)

Hailed as one of the most important jazz singers of the 20th century, Carmen Mercedes McRae was born into a West Indian family in Harlem. She studied piano and voice as a child. McRae also wrote songs from a young age. One of her songs, "Dream of Life," was recorded by Billie Holiday when McRae was still a teenager. She got her first real break as a vocalist with Benny Carter's band in 1944. She also worked with Count Basie's band and Mercer Ellington's band. Accompanying herself on piano in the early years of her career, McRae developed a signature style that was a mix of laid-back, behind-the-beat crooning and ironic deliveries of familiar lyrics. A long-time smoker, McRae retired in about 1990, due to the effects of emphysema.

ETHEL MERMAN
(1908-1984)

Ethel Agnes Zimmermann, born in Queens, New York, found fame as a singer and an actress and was known for much of her career as the "Grand Dame" of Broadway. Merman never took formal voice lessons, but had a powerful, belting mezzo-soprano voice. She came of age in the pre-microphone era, which meant she was used to filling theaters with her vocal sound without any electronic assistance. Merman began her career in vaudeville, eventually starring in several Cole Porter musicals on Broadway. Over the course of her long career, she won a Tony® and a GRAMMY and moved successfully into the worlds of film and television. Merman was married four times, including a brief marriage to Ernest Borgnine. Her most famous role was that of Gypsy Rose Lee in the musical *Gypsy*.

BETTE MIDLER
(B. 1945)

Born in Honolulu, The Divine Miss M is known as a fearless performer. Her over-the-top, belting pop renditions of songs have found her rolling onstage in a wheelchair in a mermaid costume and performing with a group of powerhouse back-up singers known as The Harlettes. Midler is also an actress. She has appeared on Broadway as well as in more than twenty-five films and more than a dozen television shows. Her varied work has brought equally varied awards, including four GRAMMY awards, three Emmy® awards, four Golden Globes®, a Tony®, Cable Ace, *TV Guide* Awards and multiple American Comedy Awards. She has also won awards for her philanthropic work, including founding the New York Restoration Project. Midler's 1990 recording of "From a Distance" hit #2 on the *Billboard* Hot 100 chart.

LIZA MINNELLI
(B. 1946)

The daughter of legendary entertainer Judy Garland and film director Victor Minnelli, Liza May Minnelli is a formidable entertainer in her own right. Minnelli won a Tony® Award at age nineteen for her role in the musical *Flora the Red Menace*, and went on to win three more. Minnelli is best known for her portrayal of Sally Bowles in the 1972 film *Cabaret*. She has won an Academy Award®, a Golden Globe®, an Emmy® and a British Academy of Film and Television Arts award. In 1990 she was honored with a GRAMMY Legend Award. Years of health problems took her off the stage for a time, but she returned in 2002 with a new concert show, *Liza's Back*. Several television appearances and a Broadway show, *Liza's at The Palace...!*, confirmed her return.

HELEN O'CONNELL
(1920-1993)

Born in Lima, Ohio, Helen O'Connell began performing with big bands in the late 1930s, getting her big break in 1939 when hired by Jimmy Dorsey. Her 1941 English language recording of "Aquellos ojos verdes" (Green Eyes) with Dorsey's orchestra spent twenty-one weeks on the charts, eventually hitting #1. *DownBeat* magazine honored O'Connell as the best female singer of both 1940 and 1941. In 1940, a *Metronome* magazine poll identified her as the best female vocalist of the year. O'Connell married in 1943 and left the business, but when her marriage ended in 1951, she returned. She made television appearances and had her own show for a time, and co-hosted the Miss Universe and Miss USA pageants from 1972-1980. O'Connell was nominated for an Emmy® in 1976 for the Miss Universe Pageant.

ANITA O'DAY (1919-2006)

Anita Belle Colton, who was born in Chicago, left home at age fourteen to dance. She eventually returned to Chicago, where bandleader Gene Krupa heard her sing and hired her for his band. She made her name as a big band singer in the 1930s and '40s, singing with the bands of Woody Herman and Stan Kenton. Unlike the majority of singers of the big band era, she changed with the styles of the times, moving to mainstream jazz in the 1950s and '60s. She was still selling out jazz clubs in the new millennium, by then in her eighties, recognized as the last of her generation of jazz singers still performing. Known as "The Jezebel of Jazz," she was as notorious for drug problems and arrests as she was famous for her one-of-a-kind voice and her speed-of-light scat singing.

PATTI PAGE (B. 1927)

Born Clara Ann Fowler in Claremore, Oklahoma, Patti Page has sold more than one hundred million records over a seven-decade career. She has charted more than one hundred songs, scored fifteen gold singles and four gold albums and one GRAMMY. Her 1950 recording of "Tennessee Waltz" hit the top spots on the pop, country and R&B charts at the same time, becoming one of the biggest-selling singles of the 20th century. She's the only singer to appear on all three major television networks. Page put elements of country music into her pop hits for many years, eventually turning her focus to country music in the 1970s. She was one of very few pre-rock era vocalists who continued to score hits after the advent of rock. Into her eighties Page was still performing about fifty concerts per year.

DIANNE REEVES (B. 1956)

Born in Detroit, Dianne Reeves grew up in Denver. She credits her uncle Charles Burrell, a bassist with the Denver Symphony, with introducing her to the music of the great jazz singers. Reeves was singing with her high school jazz band when trumpeter Clark Terry heard her and took her under his wing. She is known as one of the top jazz vocalists of her generation. She took home the "Best Jazz Vocal Album" GRAMMY in 2000, 2001, 2003 and 2005, the only singer in any category to take the award for three consecutive recordings. Reeves performed with the Lincoln Center Jazz Orchestra, the Chicago Symphony and the Orchestra of St. Luke (at Carnegie Hall) as part of the Duke Ellington Centennial Celebration and performed at the closing ceremony of the 2002 Winter Olympics in Salt Lake City.

LINDA RONSTADT
(B. 1946)

Singer and songwriter Linda Ronstadt's long career has included success in pop, Latin, country and children's music. Born in Tucson, Arizona, she has won eleven GRAMMY awards in various categories, and received another seventeen nominations. She has won an Emmy®, has been nominated for a Golden Globe® and, in 1981, was nominated for a Tony® for her work in the Broadway production of *The Pirates of Penzance*. Ronstadt, once dubbed the "Queen of Rock," has collaborated with such diverse artists as Rosemary Clooney, Phillip Glass, The Chieftains, and Frank Zappa. She has released more than thirty solo albums and has put nearly forty singles on the *Billboard* Hot 100 chart. She performed "Somewhere Out There" with James Ingram in the 1986 animated film *An American Tail*.

DINAH SHORE
(1916-1994)

Frances Rose Shore brought Southern charm to radio, to American troops in Europe during World War II, to television and to recordings. Between 1940 and 1957, the girl from Tennessee put eighty songs into the Top 40, including four that hit the #1 spot. She was one of the biggest stars of the early decades of U.S. television. Shore hosted her own show from 1951-1957, eventually spending more than thirty years on television, winning a total of five Emmy® Awards, and making the list of "most admired women in the world" on four different occasions. Shore started out singing for customers in her father's dry goods store. She got her first break when she was hired to sing on New York's WNEW radio with newcomer Frank Sinatra.

NINA SIMONE
(1933-2003)

Born Eunice Kathleen Waymon in Tryon, North Carolina, Nina Simone had dreams of becoming a classical pianist. Instead, she carved out a career as a singer, pianist, songwriter and arranger, working in a host of styles including jazz, R&B, gospel, soul, pop and classical music. Her deep, alto/tenor voice and her passionate deliveries earned her the title, "The High Priestess of Soul." Simone's concerts were often musical events that moved from style to style and found her singing, dancing, playing the piano and crusading for civil rights. Simone's 1958 debut album *Little Girl Blue* was a financial success, but not for her. Having signed away the rights for a few thousand dollars, she missed out on more than one million in royalties over the coming decades. After her death in the south of France, her ashes were scattered in several African countries.

KEELY SMITH
(B. 1932)

Dorothy Jacqueline Keely got her first paid singing gig at age fifteen. She began singing with Louis Prima in 1949 and married him in 1953. The couple had a long, successful run in Las Vegas throughout much of the 1950s. They are often credited as the inventors of the modern lounge act. She and Prima won a GRAMMY for "That Old Black Magic." Keely, who served some prison time for a drug charge, divorced Prima, remarried and retired to raise her children, making a successful comeback in 1985. Of Irish and Cherokee descent, she received the Cherokee Medal of Honor in 2000. Smith, who willingly admits that she never took a voice lesson and never learned to read music, is still active as of this writing, having played a month-long engagement at New York's Café Carlyle in April, 2007.

JO STAFFORD
(1917-2008)

California-born Jo Elizabeth Stafford is often called "America's most versatile singer." Stafford studied classical music, hoping for a career in opera. She sang in a trio with her two older sisters for a time, moving on to a vocal octet called the Pied Pipers. But it was as a solo artist that Stafford really made her mark. From the late 1930s to the mid 1960s, she recorded jazz, blues, show tunes, folk songs, Scottish songs, hymns, and big band hits. Her music was a favorite with servicemen during World War II. Stafford even ventured into comedy, with husband Paul Weston. For years the two did a parody of a bad lounge act, performing it only for friends. They eventually made a few recordings under the names Jonathan and Darlene Edwards. Stafford's bad lounge singer act won her a Best Comedy GRAMMY in 1961.

KAY STARR
(B. 1922)

Born Katherine Laverne Starks to Irish and Iroquois parents in Dougherty, Oklahoma, jazz vocalist Kay Starr grew up in Dallas. She began singing in her own backyard, serenading the chickens in their coop. The young Kay won a local radio talent contest, not once but repeatedly, until the radio station gave her a fifteen-minute radio show of her own. She continued her radio career after her parents moved the family to Memphis. At age fifteen Starr sang with Joe Venuti's band, and performed with the orchestras of Bob Crosby and Glenn Miller before returning home to finish high school. Starr scored dozens of hits throughout the 1940s and '50s, recording jazz, pop, R&B and some country tunes. She moved from recording studios to nightclubs during the British Invasion of the 1960s. She returned to the road in 1993 and recorded with Tony Bennett in 2001.

BARBRA STREISAND
(B. 1942)

Brooklyn-born Barbara Joan Streisand is one of the most successful female entertainers in history. She sings, acts, composes, produces, and directs. Her work has earned her two Academy Awards®, eight GRAMMY Awards and a Lifetime Achievement GRAMMY, four Emmy® Awards, nine Golden Globe® Awards, and the list goes on. Streisand was still a teenager when she began singing in nightclubs and appearing in a few off-Broadway shows. It was at this time that she changed the spelling of her name to the more distinctive "Barbra." She was twenty years old when she appeared in a small role in the Broadway production of *I Can Get It for You Wholesale* and signed with Columbia Records. The role of Fanny Brice in the 1964 show *Funny Girl* was written with Streisand in mind.

SARAH VAUGHAN
(1924-1990)

Growing up in Newark, New Jersey, contralto Sarah Vaughan began studying piano at age seven, eventually singing in and accompanying her church choir. In her teens, the underage Vaughan would slip into nightclubs to sit in with the bands on piano and occasionally on vocals. Vaughan won an Amateur Night competition at Harlem's famed Apollo Theater, winning ten dollars and a week's work at the theater. That week led to a gig with Earl Hines' big band at the same time Billy Eckstine was singing with the band. She was hired as a pianist, but was soon singing. Vaughan eventually left the band to follow Eckstine, who had formed his own band with jazz greats Dizzy Gillespie and Charlie Parker. One of the great singers in jazz history, Vaughan received a GRAMMY in 1982 and has had two of her recordings inducted into the Grammy Hall of Fame.

DIONNE WARWICK
(B. 1940)

Born in East Orange, New Jersey, Marie Dionne Warwick has had successful careers as a singer, actress and an ambassador. She began singing gospel as a child, first performing on television in her mid-teens, eventually earning a doctorate from the Hartt College of Music. She sang backup to numerous artists during the '60s. When Burt Bacharach heard her sing, he brought her into a partnership with himself and Hal David that would create thirty hit singles and nearly thirty albums. Warwick took their song "I'll Never Fall in Love Again," written for the musical *Promises, Promises*, to the top of the Adult Contemporary chart in 1970, winning one of her five GRAMMY awards that same year. As a social activist, she has held such positions as the United Nations Global Ambassador for the Food and Agriculture Organization.

DINAH WASHINGTON
(1924-1963)

The "Queen of the Blues" was born Ruth Lee Jones, in Alabama. Washington grew up in Chicago, where she began singing in churches. She continued to sing in churches under her own name for some time after she was established as Dinah Washington in the secular world. Washington didn't believe in mixing religion with the secular world, so she never recorded gospel music. She did record jazz, blues, R&B and pop songs, all with her emotional interpretations and powerful, high voice. Washington was married seven times, reportedly wore a mink regardless of the season or weather and was known as something of a diva in the entertainment world. The singer found a pop audience in 1959 with "Unforgettable" and "What a Diff'rence a Day Made," which earned her a GRAMMY that year. Washington was just thirty-nine when she died of an accidental drug overdose.

MARGARET WHITING
(B. 1924)

Daughter of songwriter Richard Whiting, who with Sidney Clare wrote "On the Good Ship Lollipop," Detroit-born Margaret Whiting was just seven years old when she first sang for Johnny Mercer. In 1942, she became one of the first artists he recruited for his fledgling company, Capitol Records. Whiting was one of the most important female pop singers of the 1940s and 1950s, touring with Bob Hope and Les Brown. Her career sagged with the popularity of rock. But with the 1980s came a new appreciation for the music of what has been called the "Great American Songbook," the popular songs of the pre-rock era. During the 1990s Whiting started the Eugene O'Neill Cabaret Symposium, continued recording and performing and appeared in the Broadway production of *Dream*. She is president of the Johnny Mercer Foundation and continues to perform.

NANCY WILSON
(B. 1937)

Born in Chillicothe, Ohio and raised in Columbus, singer Nancy Wilson likes to be known as a "song stylist." Not to be confused with the rock singer of the same name, Wilson has recorded more than seventy albums over the course of her career in the genres of jazz, pop, soul, blues and cabaret. She began singing professionally at age fifteen, singing in local clubs, and landed her own local television show while still in high school. She entered college, intending to become a teacher, but left to pursue a vocal career. She had her own NBC series in the late 1960s, which won her an Emmy® award, and she appeared on variety shows such as *The Carol Burnett Show*, as well as in acting roles on shows like *The Cosby Show* and *New York Undercover*. She received three GRAMMY awards, in 1964, 2004 and 2006.

ALL I COULD DO WAS CRY

Words and Music by GWEN GORDY FUQUA,
BERRY GORDY and ROQUEL DAVIS

Moderately slow, in 2

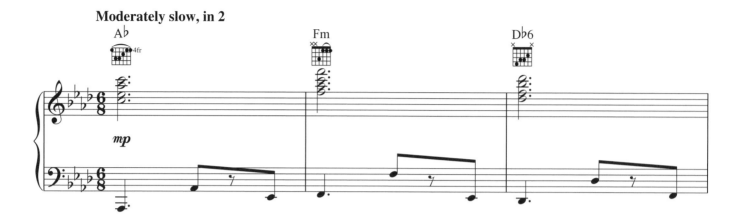

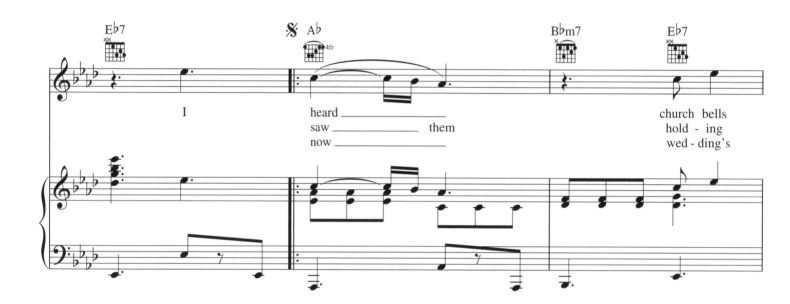

I
heard _____
saw _____ them
now _____

church bells
hold - ing
wed - ding's

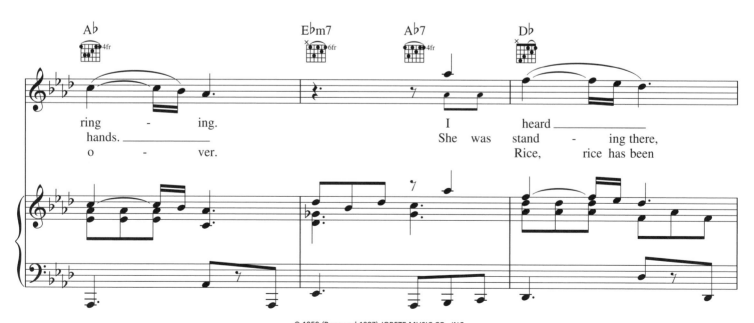

ring - ing.
hands. _____
o - ver.

I heard _____
She was stand - ing there,
Rice, rice has been

D.S. al Coda
(take 2nd ending)

AND ALL THAT JAZZ

from CHICAGO

Words by FRED EBB
Music by JOHN KANDER

AQUELLOS OJOS VERDES
(Green Eyes)

Music by NILO MENENDEZ
Spanish Words by ADOLFO UTRERA
English Words by E. RIVERA and E. WOODS

Life held no charm, dear, un-til I met you. _____
Fue - ron tus o - jos los que me die - rón _____

BABY
(You've Got What It Takes)

Words and Music by CLYDE OTIS
and MURRAY STEIN

BE ANYTHING
(But Be Mine)

Words and Music by
IRVING GORDON

Moderately slow

Be a beg-gar, be a thief, be my sun-shine or my grief, be an-y-thing, but dar-ling, be mine. _____ Be a Be a

BÉSAME MUCHO
(Kiss Me Much)

Music and Spanish Words by CONSUELO VELÁZQUEZ
English Words by SUNNY SKYLAR

Bé - sa - me, _____ bé - sa - me mu - cho, _____
Bé - sa - me, _____ *bé - sa - me mu - cho,* _____

each time I cling to your kiss I hear mu-sic di - vine. _____
co - mo si fue-ra es-ta no-che la úl-ti-ma vez; _____

Bé - sa - me mu - cho, _____
bé - sa - me mu - cho, _____

45

THE BEST IS YET TO COME

Music by CY COLEMAN
Lyrics by CAROLYN LEIGH

Out of the tree of life ___ I just picked me a plum. ___

You came a - long and ev - 'ry-thing's start - in' to

hum. ___ Still it's a real good bet ___

BLAME IT ON THE BOSSA NOVA

Words and Music by BARRY MANN
and CYNTHIA WEIL

Moderately

I was at a dance ___

when she caught my eye, ___

is my bride to be ___

stand-in' all a-lone, ___

and we're gon-na raise ___

look-in' sad and shy. ___

a fam-i-ly. ___

BUT BEAUTIFUL

from ROAD TO RIO

Words by JOHNNY BURKE
Music by JIMMY VAN HEUSEN

Love is fun-ny or it's sad, or it's
qui-et or it's mad; it's a good thing or it's
bad, but beau-ti-ful! _____

BUTTONS AND BOWS

from the Paramount Picture THE PALEFACE

Words and Music by JAY LIVINGSTON
and RAY EVANS

CABARET
from the Musical CABARET

Words by FRED EBB
Music by JOHN KANDER

CALL ME

Words and Music by
TONY HATCH

CHANGING PARTNERS

Words by JOE DARION
Music by LARRY COLEMAN

COME RAIN OR COME SHINE

from ST. LOUIS WOMAN

Words by JOHNNY MERCER
Music by HAROLD ARLEN

DADDY

Words and Music by
BOB TROUP

DEAR HEARTS AND GENTLE PEOPLE

Words by BOB HILLIARD
Music by SAMMY FAIN

DEAR RUBY
(Instrumentally known as "Ruby, My Dear")

Music by THELONIOUS MONK
Lyrics by SALLY SWISHER

DEARLY BELOVED

from YOU WERE NEVER LOVELIER

Music by JEROME KERN
Words by JOHNNY MERCER

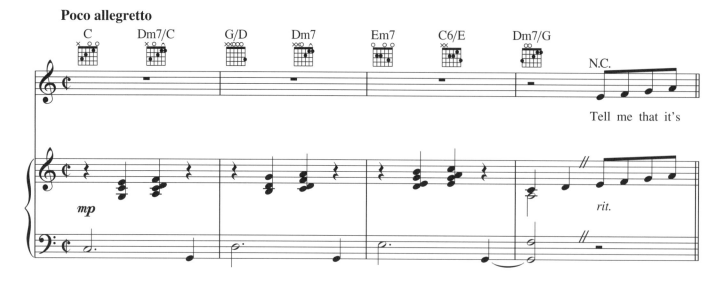

Tell me that it's

true, _____ tell me you a - gree, _____ I was meant for

you, _____ you were meant for me. _____

DON'T BE THAT WAY

Words and Music by BENNY GOODMAN,
MITCHELL PARISH and EDGAR SAMPSON

DOWNTOWN

Words and Music by
TONY HATCH

FROM A DISTANCE

Words and Music by
JULIE GOLD

EV'RY TIME WE SAY GOODBYE
from SEVEN LIVELY ARTS

Words and Music by
COLE PORTER

THE FIRST TIME EVER I SAW YOUR FACE

Words and Music by
EWAN MacCOLL

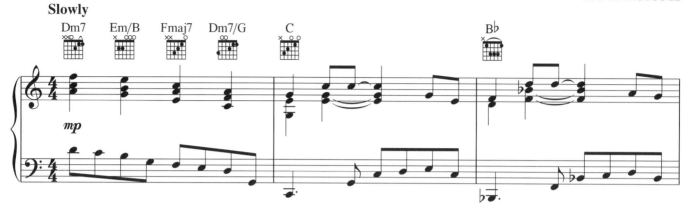

The first _ time ____
The first _ time ____
The first _ time ____

___ ev-er I saw your face, ___
___ ev-er I kissed your mouth, ___
___ ev-er I lay with you ___

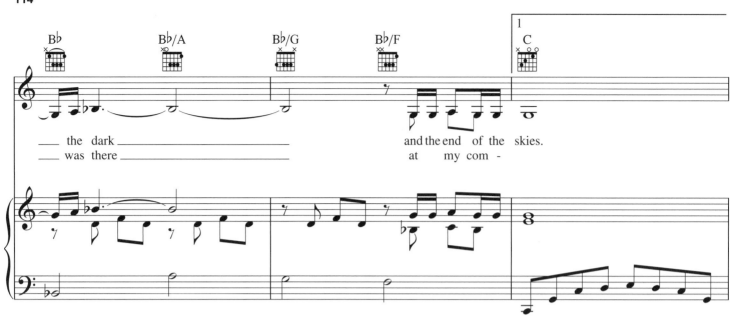

the dark _____ and the end of the skies.
was there _____ at my com -

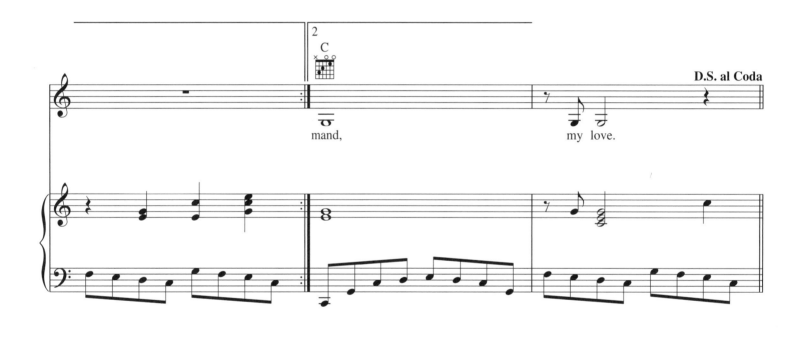

D.S. al Coda

mand, my love.

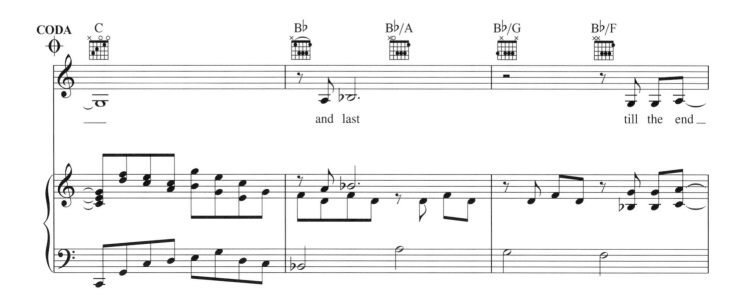

CODA

and last till the end _

THE GIRL FROM IPANEMA
(Garôta De Ipanema)

Music by ANTONIO CARLOS JOBIM
English Words by NORMAN GIMBEL
Original Words by VINICIUS DE MORAES

GOD BLESS' THE CHILD

Words and Music by ARTHUR HERZOG JR.
and BILLIE HOLIDAY

GUILTY

Words and Music by GUS KAHN,
RICHARD WHITING and HARRY AKST

GOLDEN EARRINGS

from the Paramount Picture GOLDEN EARRINGS

Words by JAY LIVINGSTON and RAY EVANS
Music by VICTOR YOUNG

A GUY IS A GUY

Words and Music by
OSCAR BRAND

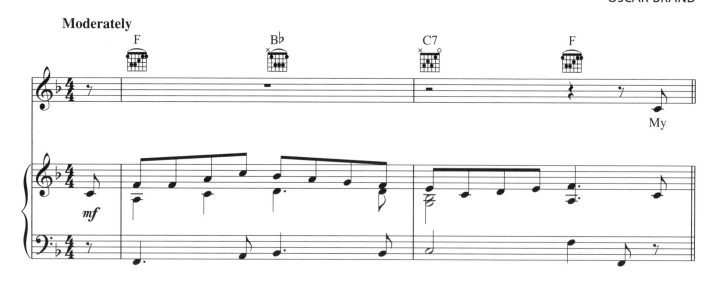

My

moth- er told me not to talk to stran- gers on the street. As years went by, re-mem-b'ring, I was
pursed my lips and tried to frown but frown-ing's not my style. I tried to pout, but what turned out? A

nev- er in- dis- creet. But, men are men and girls are girls, and men and girls are fools. We're
coy in- vit- ing smile. I'm sure he would have kissed me e- ven if I had re- fused. He

HOW HIGH THE MOON

from TWO FOR THE SHOW

Words by NANCY HAMILTON
Music by MORGAN LEWIS

I'LL GET BY
(As Long as I Have You)

Lyric by ROY TURK
Music by FRED E. AHLERT

I CAN'T BELIEVE THAT YOU'RE IN LOVE WITH ME

Words and Music by JIMMY McHUGH
and CLARENCE GASKILL

Yes - ter - day you came my way. And when you smiled at
Skies are gray, I'm blue each day. When you are not a -

me, in my heart I felt a thrill. _____ You
round, ev - 'ry - thing goes wrong, my dear, _____ I've

I'LL NEVER FALL IN LOVE AGAIN

from PROMISES, PROMISES

Lyric by HAL DAVID
Music by BURT BACHARACH

I'll never fall in love a - gain.

I'll never fall in love a - gain.

Don't tell me what it's all a - bout, 'cause

I've been there and I'm glad I'm out. Out of those chains, those

I'LL TAKE ROMANCE

Lyrics by OSCAR HAMMERSTEIN II
Music by BEN OAKLAND

I'M BEGINNING TO SEE THE LIGHT

Words and Music by DON GEORGE, JOHNNY HODGES,
DUKE ELLINGTON and HARRY JAMES

8vb

IF I WERE A BELL

from GUYS AND DOLLS

By FRANK LOESSER

I'M OLD FASHIONED

from YOU WERE NEVER LOVELIER

Words by JOHNNY MERCER
Music by JEROME KERN

IS THAT ALL THERE IS

Words and Music by JERRY LEIBER
and MIKE STOLLER

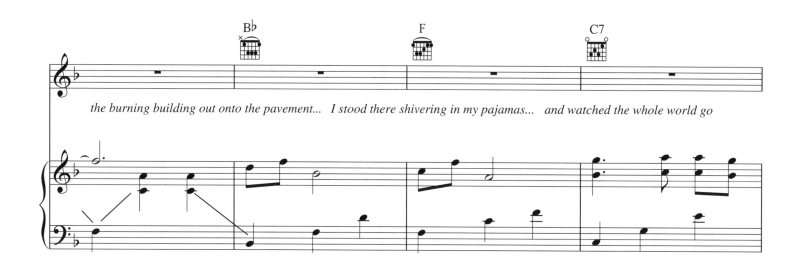

IT'S ONLY A PAPER MOON

Lyric by BILLY ROSE and E.Y. "Yip" HARBURG
Music by HAROLD ARLEN

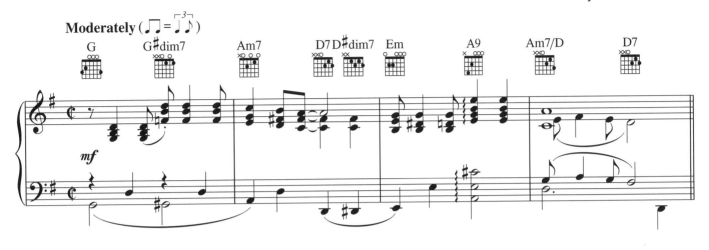

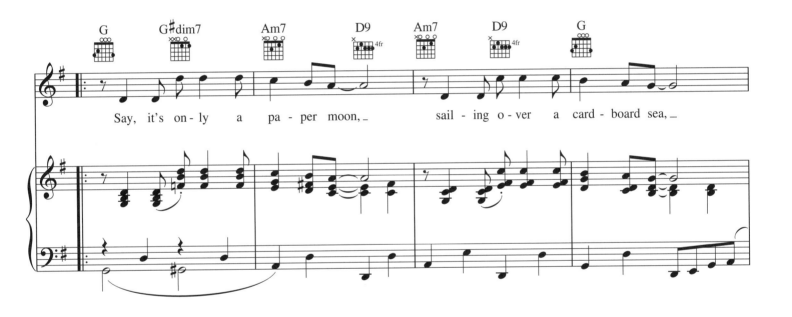

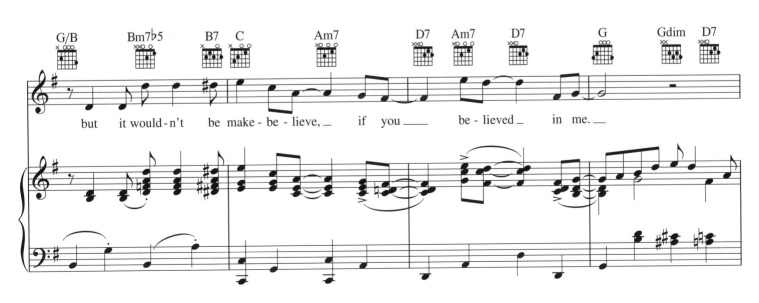

IT'S A MOST UNUSUAL DAY

from A DATE WITH JUDY

Words by HAROLD ADAMSON
Music by JIMMY McHUGH

JAMBALAYA
(On the Bayou)

Words and Music by
HANK WILLIAMS

see my ma cher a - mi - o. _____ Pick gui-

tar, fill fruit jar and be gay -o. _____ Son of a

gun, we'll have big fun on the bay - ou. _____

Thi - bo - bay - ou. _____
Set - tle

rit.

JUNE IN JANUARY

from the Paramount Picture HERE IS MY HEART

Words and Music by LEO ROBIN
and RALPH RAINGER

LITTLE GIRL BLUE

from JUMBO

Words by LORENZ HART
Music by RICHARD RODGERS

LOOK FOR THE SILVER LINING

from SALLY

Words by BUDDY DeSYLVA
Music by JEROME KERN

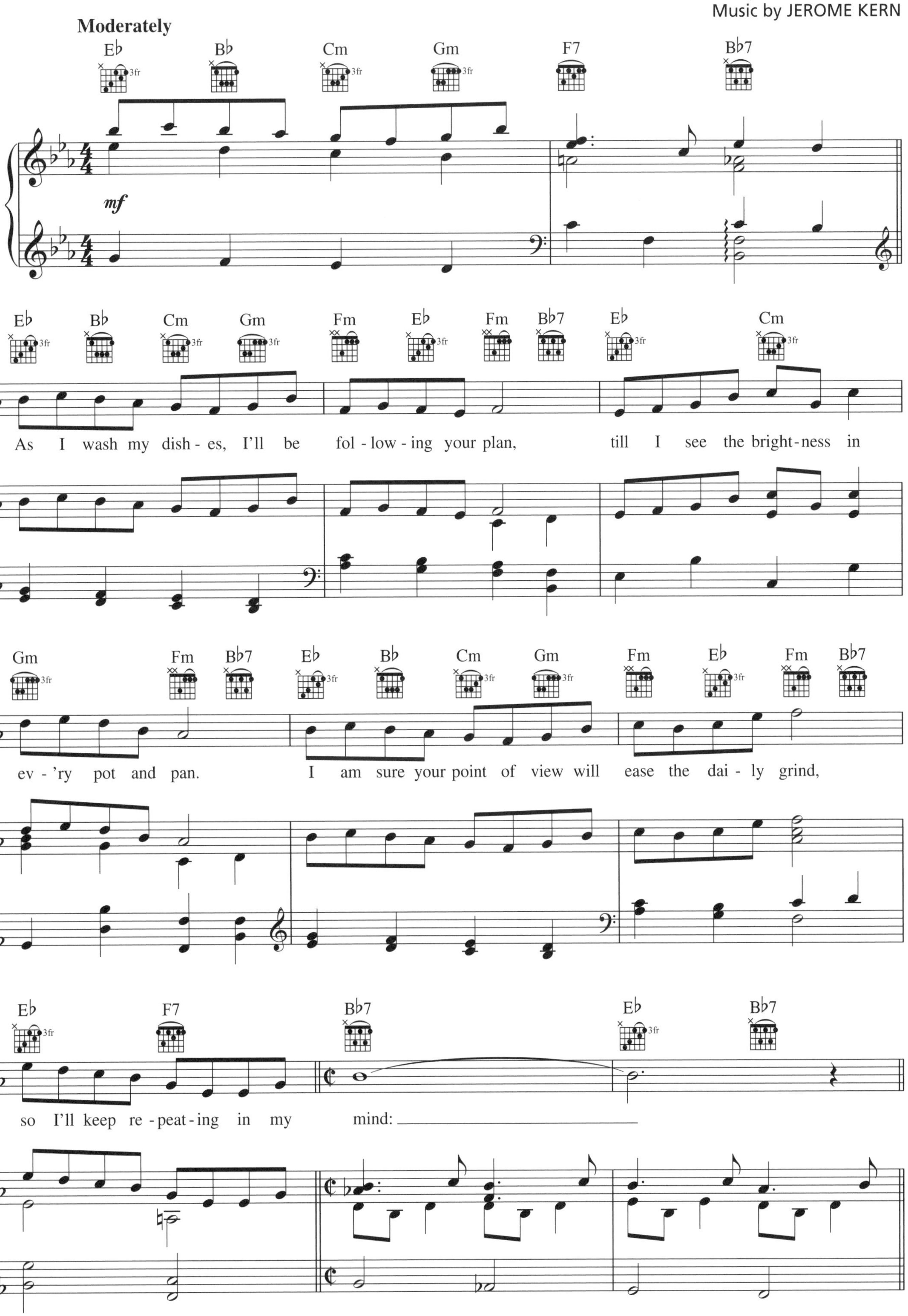

Moderately
E♭ B♭ Cm Gm F7 B♭7
mf
E♭ B♭ Cm Gm Fm E♭ Fm B♭7 E♭ Cm
As I wash my dish - es, I'll be fol - low - ing your plan, till I see the bright - ness in
Gm Fm B♭7 E♭ B♭ Cm Gm Fm E♭ Fm B♭7
ev - 'ry pot and pan. I am sure your point of view will ease the dai - ly grind,
E♭ F7 B♭7 E♭ B♭7
so I'll keep re - peat - ing in my mind:

LOVE ME OR LEAVE ME

from LOVE ME OR LEAVE ME

Lyrics by GUS KAHN
Music by WALTER DONALDSON

LOVER MAN
(Oh, Where Can You Be?)

By JIMMY DAVIS,
ROGER RAMIREZ and JIMMY SHERMAN

pray'r that you'll make love to me, strange as it seems,

some day we'll meet and you'll dry all my tears, ___ then whis-per sweet lit-tle

things in my ears, ___ hug-gin' and a kiss-in', oh, what we've been miss-in'.

Lov-er man, oh where can you be? be?

LULLABY OF BIRDLAND

Words by GEORGE DAVID WEISS
Music by GEORGE SHEARING

MANGOS

Words and Music by DEE LIBBEY
and SID WAYNE

* Recorded a half step lower.

MEMORIES OF YOU

Lyric by ANDY RAZAF
Music by EUBIE BLAKE

MISTY

Words by JOHNNY BURKE
Music by ERROLL GARNER

MY FUNNY VALENTINE
from BABES IN ARMS

Words by LORENZ HART
Music by RICHARD RODGERS

(There Ought to Be A)
MOONLIGHT SAVINGS TIME

Words and Music by IRVING KAHAL
and HARRY RICHMAN

MY HEART BELONGS TO ONLY YOU

Words and Music by FRANK DANIELS
and DOROTHY DANIELS

Lyrics:

My heart be-longs to on - ly you, I've nev - er loved as

I love you, you've set a flame with - in me burn-ing,

a flame to stay with - in me yearn - ing. It's just for you I

MY SHINING HOUR
from the Motion Picture THE SKY'S THE LIMIT

Lyric by JOHNNY MERCER
Music by HAROLD ARLEN

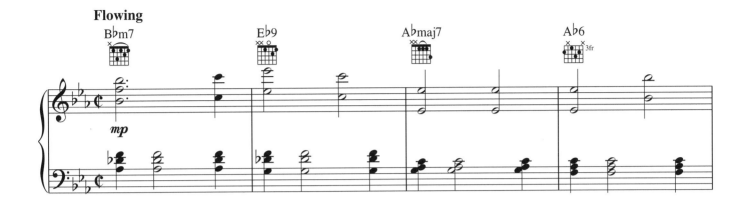

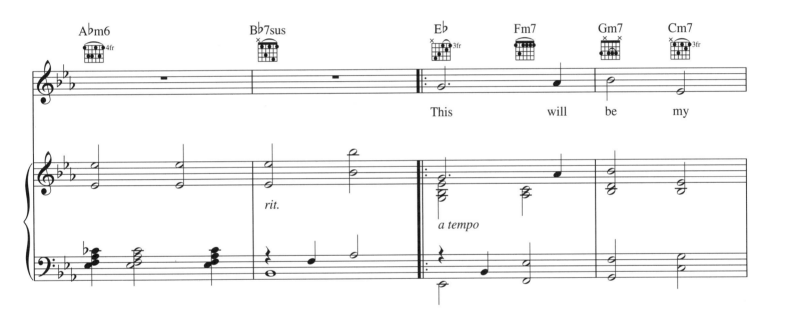

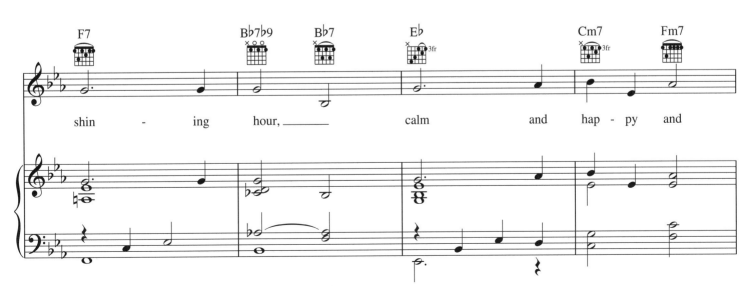

NIGHT SONG

from GOLDEN BOY

Lyric by LEE ADAMS
Music by CHARLES STROUSE

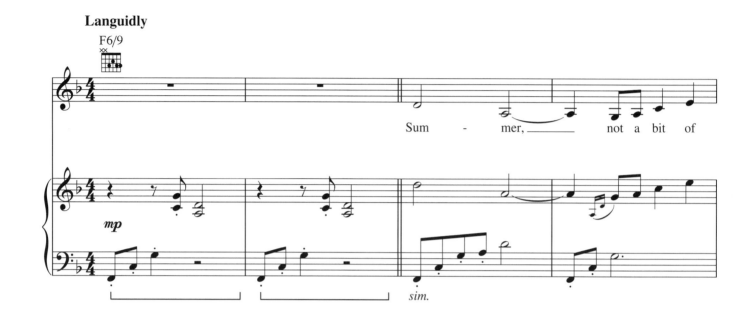

ONE FOR MY BABY
(And One More for the Road)
from the Motion Picture THE SKY'S THE LIMIT

Lyric by JOHNNY MERCER
Music by HAROLD ARLEN

SHRIMP BOATS

Words and Music by PAUL MASON HOWARD
and PAUL WESTON

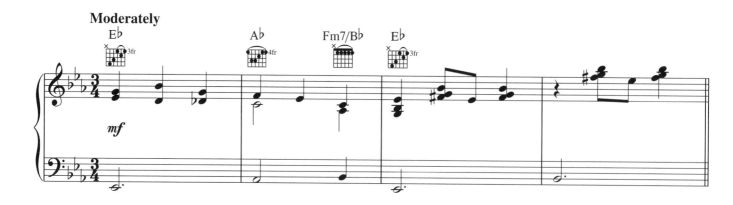

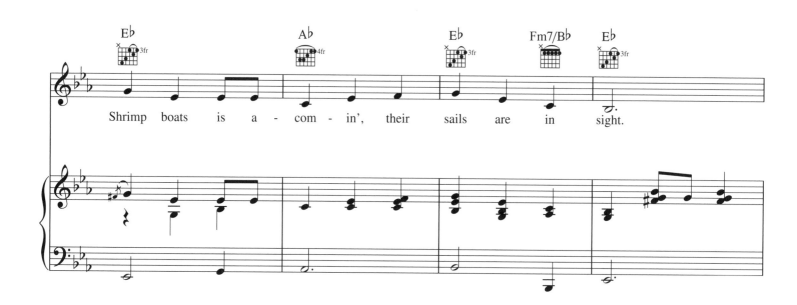

Shrimp boats is a - com - in', their sails are in sight.

Shrimp boats is a - com - in', there's danc - in' to - night. Why don't-cha

SOMEWHERE OUT THERE
from AN AMERICAN TAIL

Music by BARRY MANN and JAMES HORNER
Lyric by CYNTHIA WEIL

Moderately, with expression

Some - where out there, be - neath the pale moon -

light, some - one's think - in' of me and

STARDUST

Words by MITCHELL PARISH
Music by HOAGY CARMICHAEL

And now the pur-ple dusk of twi-light time

steals a-cross the mead-ows of my heart.

High up in the sky the

lit-tle stars climb,

al-ways re-mind-ing me that

But that was long a- go: now my con- so- la - tion is

in the star- dust of a song. Be - side a gar- den

wall, when stars are bright, you are in my arms. The

night- in- gale tells his fair- y tale of par - a - dise, where ros - es

THE SONG IS ENDED
(But the Melody Lingers On)

Words and Music by
IRVING BERLIN

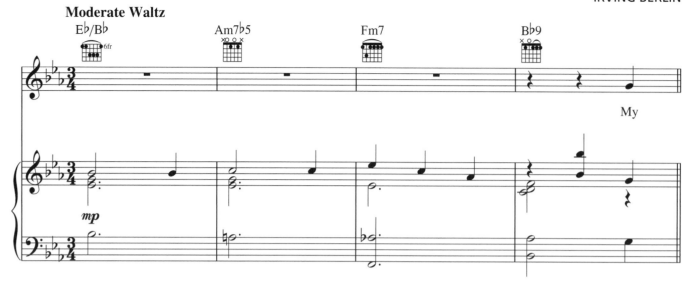

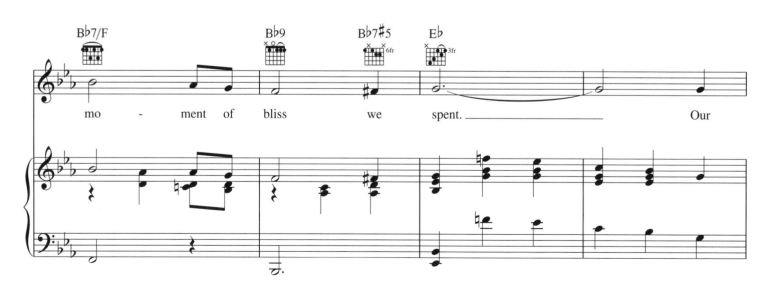

STORMY WEATHER
(Keeps Rainin' All the Time)

from COTTON CLUB PARADE OF 1933
featured in the Motion Picture STORMY WEATHER

Lyric by TED KOEHLER
Music by HAROLD ARLEN

Interlude

A SUNDAY KIND OF LOVE

Words and Music by LOUIS PRIMA,
ANITA NYE, STAN RHODES
and BARBARA BELLE

TENNESSEE WALTZ

Words and Music by REDD STEWART
and PEE WEE KING

duced him to my loved one and ____ while they were ____

waltz - ing my friend stole my sweet - heart from

me. ____ I re - mem - ber the

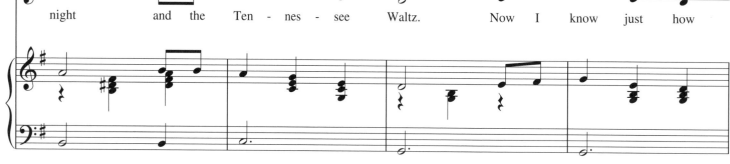

night and the Ten - nes - see Waltz. Now I know just how

THERE'S NO BUSINESS LIKE SHOW BUSINESS

from the Stage Production ANNIE GET YOUR GUN

Words and Music by
IRVING BERLIN

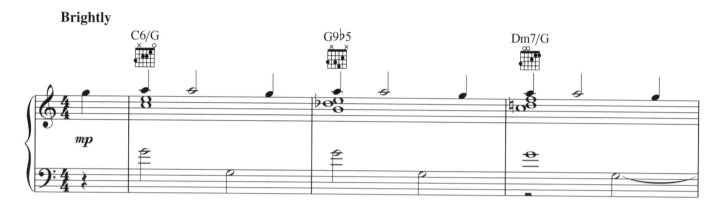

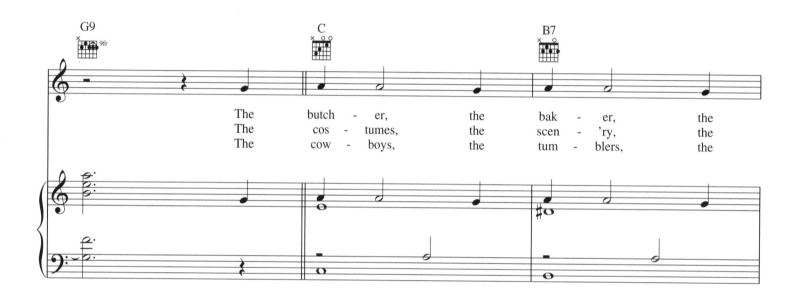

The butch- er, the bak- er, the
The cos- tumes, the scen- 'ry, the
The cow- boys, the tum- blers, the

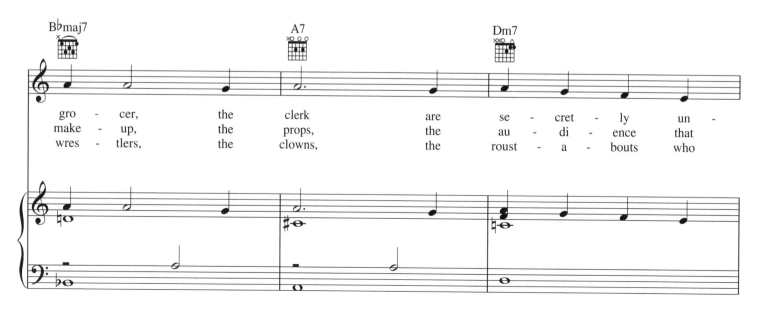

gro- cer, the clerk are se- cret- ly un-
make- up, the props, the au- di- ence that
wres- tlers, the clowns, the roust- a- bouts who

THEY SAY IT'S WONDERFUL

from the Stage Production ANNIE GET YOUR GUN

Words and Music by
IRVING BERLIN

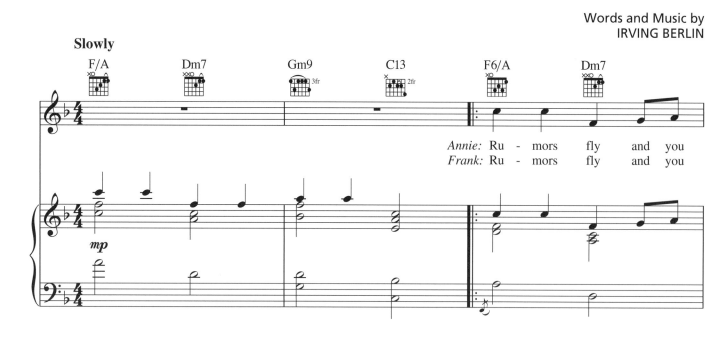

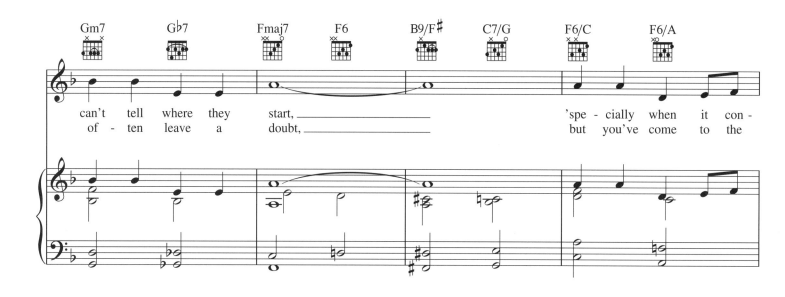

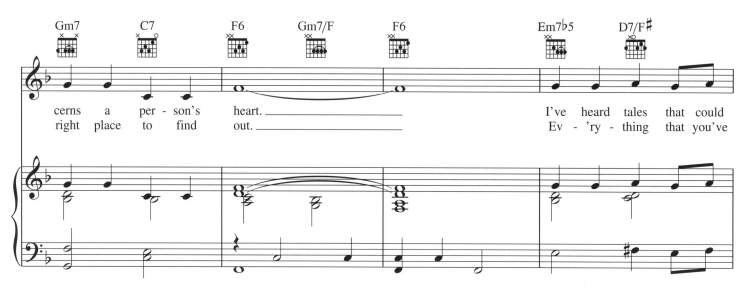

THIS WILL BE
(An Everlasting Love)

Words and Music by MARVIN YANCY
and CHUCK JACKSON

UNFORGETTABLE

Words and Music by
IRVING GORDON

THE WAY WE WERE

from the Motion Picture THE WAY WE WERE

Words by ALAN and MARILYN BERGMAN
Music by MARVIN HAMLISCH

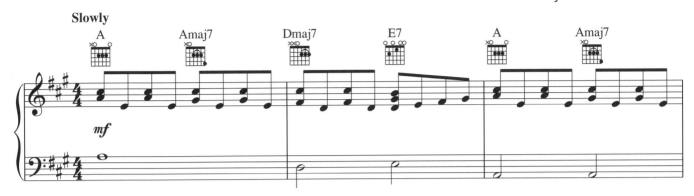

VIOLETS FOR YOUR FURS

By TOM ADAIR
and MATT DENNIS

by. You smiled at me so sweet - ly; since then one thought oc - curs, that we fell in love com - plete - ly the day that

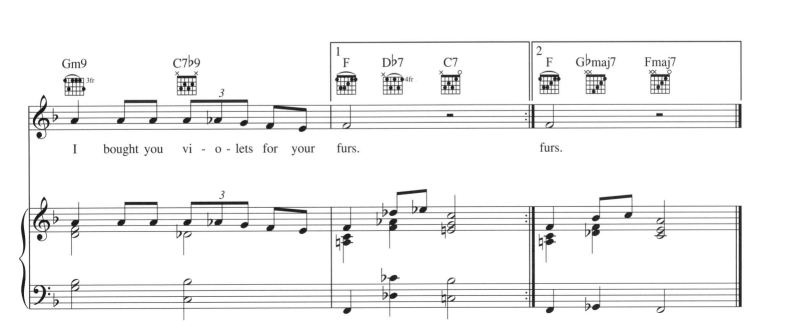

I bought you vi - o - lets for your furs. furs.

WHEEL OF FORTUNE

Words and Music by BENNIE BENJAMIN
and GEORGE WEISS

Slowly and expressively

WHY DON'T YOU BELIEVE ME

Words and Music by LEW DOUGLAS,
LUTHER KING LANEY and LEROY W. RODDE

WIVES AND LOVERS
(Hey, Little Girl)
from the Paramount Picture WIVES AND LOVERS

Words by HAL DAVID
Music by BURT BACHARACH

YOU'LL NEVER WALK ALONE

from CAROUSEL

Lyrics by OSCAR HAMMERSTEIN II
Music by RICHARD RODGERS

* alternate lyric: hold your head up high